W9-AYD-993

THE WORLDS OF ARCHITECTURAL DIGEST

THE COLLECTORS

THE WORLDS OF ARCHITECTURAL DIGEST

THE COLLECTORS

EDITED BY PAIGE RENSE

EDITOR-IN-CHIEF, ARCHITECTURAL DIGEST

THE KNAPP PRESS   PUBLISHERS   LOS ANGELES

Published in the United States of America in 1982
The Knapp Press
5900 Wilshire Boulevard, Los Angeles, California 90036
Copyright © 1982 by Knapp Communications Corporation
All rights reserved
First Edition

Distributed by The Viking Press
625 Madison Avenue, New York, New York 10022

Distributed simultaneously in Canada by Penguin Books Canada Limited

Library of Congress Cataloging in Publication Data
Main entry under title: The Collectors.
(The Worlds of Architectural digest)
Selections from the pages of Architectural digest,
newly edited and designed.
1. Art—Private collections. 2. Antiques in interior decoration.
I. Rense, Paige. II. Architectural digest
III. Series.
N5210.C59   1982   709'.2'2   82-8970
AACR2

ISBN 0-89535-103-X
Printed and bound in the United States of America

CONTENTS

FOREWORD

The desire to be surrounded by beautiful art and antiques is one of man's most civilized impulses. Throughout history, people of taste, knowledge and refinement have created collections to elevate their spirits and those of their fellowman. Certainly all of the great museum collections that add such delight to our lives are indebted to the incalculable generosity of private collectors. Yet, for every treasure on public view, many more, of comparable quality, remain tucked away in the great private collections of the world. One of my special pleasures as editor-in-chief of ARCHITECTURAL DIGEST is sharing these treasures with our readers by taking them into the homes of some of the most discerning private collectors of our time.

Not only do "The Collectors" features spotlight works of art, antiques and artifacts, they also offer intriguing insights into the lives of the collectors themselves, and how they incorporate their collections into fine interior designs.

As you will see in the pages that follow, the design solutions are as varied and dynamic as the collectors themselves. The late Marjorie Merriweather Post's *Hillwood*, for example, re-creates the splendor of imperial Russia with French antique furnishings, Fabergé objets d'art, exquisite porcelains and royal portraiture. In contrast, the Manhattan apartment of artist Fred Wehmer is far more intimate in mood. Simply appointed with very fine examples of Biedermeier furniture, it has the cozy air of Vienna in the 1830s. On the island of Majorca, Don Bartolomé March has assembled his outstanding collection of modern sculpture in a unique setting—a colorful garden resplendent with flowering bougainvillea. And in Connecticut,

Helen Partello-Hollingsworth has made a fine collection of American primitive furniture, folk art and artifacts an integral part of her charming 1790 farmhouse.

As divergent as these collections are, they and the others in this volume share several characteristics. Perhaps most evident of all is their selectivity: each collector has approached his or her subject with intelligence and taste, two key elements of true connoisseurship. It comes as no surprise to find that the designs of their homes also reflect this same fine sense of discrimination. What impresses me most, however, is the devotion shown by these collectors—a devotion that comes from their passion for beauty and their desire to make it an essential part of their daily lives.

Paige Rense
Editor-in-Chief
Los Angeles, California

THE WORLDS OF ARCHITECTURAL DIGEST

THE COLLECTORS

RICHES OF THE CZARS

The Baroque palaces of Leningrad seem a far distance from a neo-Georgian mansion on a twenty-four-acre estate in Washington, D.C. Yet among the treasures in the nation's capital, none are so fabulous as the collections from imperial Russia housed at *Hillwood*, once the home of the late Marjorie Merriweather Post. Here, the spirit and magnificence of the Russian czars live again in rooms specially built to display innumerable dazzling objects, gathered over the years by a woman with a taste for rarity and opulence. Mrs. Post was the only child of Charles William Post, the breakfast cereal magnate, and as his sole heir she demonstrated an energy and astuteness to match her father's.

Mrs. Post's way of life paralleled her great wealth. She maintained a number of homes, where she entertained presidents and princes on an awesome scale. In addition to her fame as a hostess, her extraordinary vigor allowed her the time not only to head a colossal business enterprise but also to pursue her many philanthropies, while assembling both the Russian collection and examples of the finest French eighteenth-century furniture, *objets*, royal Sèvres porcelain and Beauvais tapestries. Both collections are lodged at Hillwood, which she acquired in 1955 with the express purpose of transforming the house, built some thirty years before, into a home and museum to display her collections. Under her guidance, rooms were added and the grounds were landscaped to include a charming French parterre, a Japanese garden and a dacha—the Russian equivalent of a country house—as well as a large greenhouse to cultivate her favorite flower, the orchid. The estate and collections are now administered by the Marjorie Merriweather Post Foundation, and just as she had planned, in July 1977 Hillwood was opened as a museum.

In 1927, Mrs. Post acquired from the Yussupov collection a brilliant Fabergé snuffbox fashioned from one piece of amethyst quartz, set with emeralds and diamonds—the lid a sleeping dog carved in ruby matrix. It was Prince Felix Yussupov who murdered Rasputin, in December 1916, and his large private art collection was nationalized at the time of the Russian Revolution. A celebrated pink imperial Easter egg, made by Carl Fabergé and given by Czar Nicholas II to his mother in 1914, was added in 1931. Then, in an enviable piece of timing, Mrs. Post was in Moscow in 1937 and 1938 as the wife of then United States ambassador, the Honorable Joseph E. Davies. At this moment the Soviet regime threw open to the diplomatic community warehouses full of confiscated treasures from the palaces of the czars and the Russian churches. Among the jumbled heaps of glorious objects Mrs. Post found rare chalices dating from the seventeenth century, religious vestments embroidered in silver and gold, early porcelains, and the very imposing ebony cabinet decorated with ormolu and inset with lapis lazuli that now stands in the icon room at Hillwood. This event stimulated Mrs. Post's interest in Russian decorative arts, and she amassed a unique collection that is said to have no equivalent outside of Russia.

Here at Hillwood, facing Washington's lovely Rock Creek Park, a past long gone has been preserved with love and affection. For, although Mrs. Post's opulent way of life has quite vanished, and guests are no longer greeted by liveried footmen, that sense of what she called "old-fashioned elegance" still suffuses Hillwood. In its richly decorative collections are suspended for eternity not only Mrs. Post's zest for living but the elegance and style of France's *belle époque* and the romance, barbarism and splendor of Russia's imperial past.

Hillwood, the Washington, D.C. home of the late Marjorie Merriweather Post, houses her collection of objects from imperial Russia. PRECEDING PAGE: Dominating the Main Hallway is a formal portrait, attributed to Levitzky, of Catherine the Great. LEFT: In the French Drawing Room, vitrines display Sèvres porcelain dinnerware. The portrait of the Empress Eugénie is by Winterhalter. ABOVE: A portrait by Nattier in the French Drawing Room depicts the duchess of Parma and her daughter. The swivel chair and roll-top desk originally belonged to Marie Antoinette.

5

LEFT: *The Russian Porcelain Room displays a superlative collection, including four dinner services used by Catherine the Great when entertaining the knights of her imperial orders.* BELOW LEFT: *A bay window banked with orchids lends the Breakfast Room a winter garden air. The handsome chandelier was made especially for the palace at Tsarskoe Selo.*

ABOVE: *In the Dining Room, Régence boiserie and an Aubusson rug establish a formal context for a large pietra dura dining table. Contributing ornate detail are a 19th-century commode and a pair of Italian Rococo consoles. Boiserie frames paintings by Dirk Langendyk.* FOLLOWING PAGES: *Constantin Makovsky's painting* The Boyar Wedding *is a focal point of the Pavilion Room, designed to serve as both gallery and theater. Appointed with small settees, crystal lamps and vitrines filled with* objets de vertu, *the room is both classical and Russian in style.*

LEFT: *Russian censers and gold and silver chalices make up one of Hillwood's collections.* BELOW LEFT: *Silk-damask-covered walls brilliant with icons, a vitrine displaying imperial Russian Easter eggs, and a cabinet of ebony, ormolu and lapis lazuli give the Icon Room a jewel-box-like appearance.* OPPOSITE TOP: *Although the Imperial nuptial crown is encrusted with diamonds, the pride of Hillwood is the collection of tion of Fabergé imperial Easter eggs; complementing the eggs is Mrs. Post's first Russian acquisition—a Fabergé snuffbox.* OPPOSITE: *In the Empire Room an Austrian wallhanging surmounts an ornate 19th-century heraldic Empire bed.*

MODERN EXUBERANCE

Looking out from fashion designer Arnold Scaasi's apartment high on the cliff of Central Park South, few can resist rhapsodizing over the beautiful view of Central Park's 840-acre sweep. To Mr. Scaasi, The Park—and the word can mean only one place to Manhattanites—is very special, very beautiful, very much of their city. It is a magic amalgam of picnickers, earnest bicyclists and kite flyers. These are all pure New York, and pure delight when surveyed from this unique apartment sitting high over the South American "libertadores" whose equestrian monuments cavort tirelessly at the south edge of the park. Everything in the apartment is geared to the view and drenched in waves of north light that roll through the double-story studio windows. Visual relationships are dominant. The eye moves from living room to loggia, back down to the park and up again to the windows that give even the back bedroom a splendid view of the outdoors.

Art is a basic ingredient in the apartment and it is very much a part of Arnold Scaasi's life. The paintings in his collection are shown to advantage in the living room with its studio atmosphere of north light, bare oak floors, a loggia, white walls and twenty-foot ceilings; they even look as if they could have been painted there. The vital forms and dynamic colors of a Fernand Léger, the intellectually structured vision of a Jean Metzinger, the animated abstraction of a Futurist Giacomo Balla and the sensuality of a large Picasso all cohabit in perfect harmony. They are presided over by a Louise Nevelson assemblage above the Renaissance fireplace and the unique, unexpected delight of Nevelson's only ceiling piece, made specially for the loggia.

Arnold Scaasi is a man of self-assurance and acumen, with the matching courage to do and have whatever he likes. "I'm very visual, and I want every-thing to be pretty, exciting and warm, rather than hard and cold," he explains. "To me, the project of designing is inseparable from the project of living. You reconstruct your life from time to time, and so reconstruct all the objects around you." When he took the Central Park South apartment, he knew he wanted it to be luxurious and comfortable but not excessive. That's not the way he thinks, and that's not the way he lives. He relies on his eye and on his own feelings. In his present apartment he felt that certain rooms should be exciting, because they are not in constant use; dining rooms and entrance halls, for instance, should shock the senses and create fantasy. He also believes in having an "almost throwaway room, a pictorial thing," like the open, mirrored but sparsely furnished loggia. It is a special, privileged place, a quietly magical eyrie for viewing the city below and the Nevelson ceiling above.

Successful as the apartment is, Arnold Scaasi sees few relationships between his career as a leading fashion designer and the art of interior design. "In a way, though, I design interiors as I do a collection. I make a master plan first. But then I have to see it, and if it doesn't work I'm open to change. You begin by paring an interior down to essentials, and then you ornament it to please your eye. In that, it's like fashion design. Your own eye tells you when a change should take place, but it takes a very good eye to find the exact placement that looks right. However, once you have it, it will never look right any other way." Looking about his living room, he adds, "This room is perfect to my eye. For me that's the best way." In this spacious apartment, with its remarkable works of art and its view of the park below, Arnold Scaasi feels comfortable, and he makes his friends feel comfortable as well. Both of these are major, and felicitous, accomplishments.

PRECEDING PAGE: *In the Living Room of fashion designer Arnold Scaasi's New York apartment, a Louise Nevelson assemblage emphasizes the lofty proportions of the space. Flanking it are, to the left,* Elements mécaniques, *a 1919 work by Fernand Léger, and* Nature morte, *circa 1930, by Jean Metzinger.* ABOVE: *An Ernest Trova reclining figure rests on a tabletop in the Living Room. The painting is by Paul Jenkins.*

ABOVE: *From an interior window of the master bedroom, the designer can look across his Living Room to Central Park.* OPPOSITE: *In the Loggia, an 18th-century head, ringed by anemones and crowned with acrylic snakes, enhances an intimate tablesetting. Glowing candles reiterate the distant sparkle of the Manhattan cityscape.*

14

ABOVE: *Images multiply in the mirrored Master Bedroom. At right is Ernest Trova's* **Mechanical Man.** OPPOSITE: *Mr. Scaasi believes that the Dining Room, used infrequently, should inspire fantasy. "I wanted a room to show off my Dubuffet* Vacanciers." *The sculpture is by Gio Pomodoro.*

QUEEN ELIZABETH II

In England there is no equivalent of Versailles, and it is important to stress that point. At a time when almost every European sovereign was paying homage to the memory of Louis XIV by building miniature versions of Versailles, the English royal family's palaces were private houses. Buckingham Palace was simply renamed The Queen's House when George III bought it in 1761. However, George IV had more grandiose ideas. When he came to the throne in 1821, he immediately began to rebuild The Queen's House in almost its present form, and restored the palace's original name. Even so, he told his architect, John Nash, that he simply wanted his mother's former residence turned "into a private house for myself." Today Buckingham Palace is, in an almost literal way, The Queen's House —the home of Queen Elizabeth II and her family.

Things might have been quite different if the English had not turned the Stuarts off the throne in 1688 and replaced them with the more democratically minded Dutchman, William of Orange. His Dutch upbringing caused the new king to prefer less flamboyant decorations, and he handed down more modest tastes to his Hanoverian successors. The first two of them left little impression on the furnishings of the royal palaces, but George III and George IV made deeper marks. However, their acquisitions were as strikingly different as their characters. George III and Queen Charlotte, in fact, led a life of such bourgeois domesticity that they awakened derision among the smarter members of society and even became the butt of caricaturists. On the other hand, the extravagance of the Prince of Wales equally annoyed his contemporaries.

As a young prince, the future George IV already found Parisian fashion more to his taste than its English equivalent. And his London residence, *Carl-ton House,* was furnished at very great expense by Dominique Daguerre, the most fashionable furniture dealer in Paris. Actually the outbreak of the French Revolution greatly increased the future English king's opportunity to buy furniture from abroad, for the aristocratic refugees brought their furniture with them from France to London, later selling much of it to provide money. And in 1793 the revolutionary government of France auctioned off the contents of the former royal palaces, so the opportunities to acquire the best French eighteenth-century furniture increased even more, since most of it came to the English market. But the Prince Regent, as he became during the period of George III's insanity, also had a number of agents in Paris acquiring furniture and works of art. The prince himself haunted London sale rooms and antique shops with his friend the marquess of Hertford. A man with similar tastes, the marquess laid the foundations of what is now the Wallace Collection.

The extent of George IV's French furniture today in Queen Elizabeth's collections at Buckingham Palace is consequently enormous. For example, the monumental jewel cabinet made by Jean Henri Riesener for the comtesse de Provence, sister-in-law of Louis XVI; the major furnishings of Louis XVI's bedchamber at Versailles; the rolltop desk made by the *ébéniste* Teuné in 1782 for the comte d'Artois, the future King Charles X; the so-called Negress Head clock—the list seems endless. Until his death in 1829, George IV collected avidly. The result was that within his lifetime he made the English Royal Collection the only serious rival to the prestigious Wallace Collection itself. And many of the works of art that George IV collected remain carefully preserved in Buckingham Palace—today, perhaps more accurately than ever before, The Queen's House.

At Buckingham Palace and Windsor Castle, Her Majesty
Queen Elizabeth II is surrounded by superlative examples
of 18th-century furniture. PRECEDING PAGE: *A bureau à
cylindre was made by François-Gaspard Teuné in 1782
for Louis XVI's younger brother.* ABOVE: *Brilliantly colored
inlaid panels of* pietra dura *decorate an ebony-veneered
commode by the Parisian ébéniste Martin Carlin.*

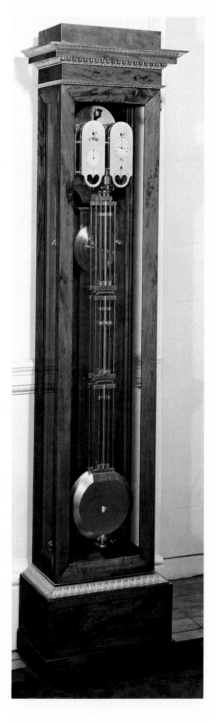

ABOVE LEFT: *The glass-paneled mahogany double-pendulum clock by Abraham-Louis Breguet was purchased by George IV in 1825. Considered a horological masterpiece, it features two compensating movements.* ABOVE: *Around 1700, the citizens of London presented King William III and Queen Mary with a glittering solid silver side table and mirror crafted by London silversmith Andrew Moore.*

TOP: *Pictorial marquetry embellishes an elaborate commode by Jean Henri Riesener, originally delivered in 1774 to Louis XVI.* ABOVE: *A mechanically opening globe-shaped table rests on satyr standards. Queen Charlotte acquired the ingenious object in 1809 from Morgan and Saunders, who had purchased the patent from George Remington.*

TOP: *Riesener made the mahogany veneer and gilt-bronze jewel cabinet for the comtesse de Provence, sister-in-law of Louis XVI. Both pieces by Riesener were purchased by George IV at auction in 1825.* ABOVE: *Queen Charlotte's jewel cabinet, supplied in 1761 by Vile and Cobb, is veneered with a number of different exotic woods.*

The pewter marquetry writing bureau on display
at Windsor Castle was made for William III and Mary
in 1695 by the Dutch cabinetmaker Gerreit Jensen.

23

NUANCES OF HISTORY

Perched atop a hill on the southern side of Athens is a house that commands a spectacular view across the ancient city to both the sea and the Acropolis. Built for a discriminating client by American architect Charles Shoup in typical Athenian Neo-Classic style, the airy and voluminous rooms of the residence are filled with a remarkable collection of ancient artifacts that blend with French Directoire and Empire, English Classical and Russian Neo-Classical furniture. An uneasy mixture of republican austerity and symbolistic imperial ornament characterizes the Neo-Classic style, often making it all but unlivable. Apparently born of a loveless mating of Doric rigidity and late-Georgian English coldness, its severely logical aesthetic can be frigid and abstract in extreme isolation. Nevertheless, the tripods, trophies, urns, cameos, volutes, lozenges, lyres and assorted winged creatures of Neo-Classicism offer a fascinating decorative vocabulary.

The resident, a distinguished collector, has brilliantly—and perhaps brashly—contrived to subvert the overly solemn aims of Neo-Classic design by upholstering furniture in colorful ethnic embroideries and covering floors with the powerful geometrics of Middle Eastern tribal rugs. The extensive use of ethnic embroideries alters and relaxes the tone of the Neo-Classic furniture without disguising its origins. The tribal rugs actively articulate and anchor the apparently contradictory styles found in the interiors, where the variety of objects and the orchestration of unrelated styles are the only constants. The cornucopia is abundant: from the entrance, with its Empire console holding Roman carvings and part of an Italian Renaissance baptistery and its paintings of heroes of the Greek War of Independence, to Directoire pieces covered in Bukhara embroideries in the living room and master bedroom; from the Russian Neo-Classic sofa in the library, upholstered in Moroccan silk caftan material, to cushions covered in Attic embroideries, and on to pre-Dynastic Egyptian pots; from Middle Eastern kilims to brightly embroidered Indian bedcovers guarded by winged-sphinx headboards.

Moving to Athens from Paris, the resident left most of his furniture behind. As Charles Shoup puts it, "my client wanted Greece with all its historical allusions." He wanted, too, its climate and a good deal of space, where everything could be on a large, expansive scale. The architect was asked to create spaces ranging from a "monumental entrance for what suddenly became a very grand flat" to an opulent octagonal bathroom, which Mr. Shoup describes as "a dream, like some fantastic Turkish bath." It took three years to build the residence, since everything down to the smallest detail was custom-made to suit this unique and special house.

Amidst elegance and luxurious comfort, there is understatement everywhere, mixed with a penchant for very large and unusual things. "My client," the architect explains, "is very fond of the oversized. It's a special taste. He did his interiors in a way I wouldn't have expected. He acquires oversize things and many other kinds of objects—a bit of a temple, an ancient urn—but it all works. Only he would have done it quite that way, but every time I come in I say 'Bravo!'" The great French painter Jacques Louis David, who did so much to introduce Neo-Classicism to France, stated clearly that antique art is lifeless and without "seduction"—unless "seasoned with a modern sauce." Here, in so sensitive a collection, this sauce has been used generously but judiciously, creating a home animated by the souvenirs of history, where the wiles of culture and the juggled nuances of style can very easily seduce.

PRECEDING PAGE: *The Classical Revival flavor of an Athens residence is created by expansive architecture, collections of artifacts and a mixture of period furnishings. In the Entrance Hall, a Neo-Classic coffered ceiling, pilasters and a marble floor provide a hard-surface framework. The Empire console displays Roman vases and a* modello *for the dome of an Italian Renaissance baptistery. An early-19th-century portrait of a Greek war hero animates the space.* RIGHT: *In the Living Room, a bold Charles X rug and small 19th-century Tibetan prayer rugs anchor the diverse assembly, while colorful ethnic upholstery, such as the old Bukhara fabric covering an Empire curule stool, lightens the Neo-Classic formality of the décor.*

A number of Living Room arrangements promote the aesthetic intermin-
gling of artworks and antiquities.
Groups of archaeological objects displayed on Neo-Classic tables give the
effect of telescoping the centuries.

ABOVE: *A Regency étagère presents
predynastic Egyptian vases. Paintings,
at left, render views of the Acropolis.
Beneath a Neo-Classic mirror, a marble and porphyry mantel, circa 1800,
displays the head of Hermes.*

28

TOP: *Roman sculpture and predynastic Egyptian vases rest on a Louis XVI folding table. The painting of Turkish musicians is 18th century.* ABOVE: *An English portrait dates from the mid-19th century. Beneath it, a Roman marble vase graces the commode.*

TOP: *Roman glass objects cluster on a slate-topped bronze table, a French Directoire copy of a Roman original.* ABOVE: *An Italian table complements an English chair, both circa 1800. A French painting, from the same period, contributes a heroic motif.*

29

TOP: *Potted plants soften the Neo-Classic architecture of the second-floor Hall. A set of engravings, circa 1790, depict the Vatican Museum.* TOP RIGHT: *Antique Italian landscape paintings adorn a Guest Room.* ABOVE: *Late-19th-century Italian plaster medallions, representing the Four Seasons, and a Roman lion's-head fountain embellish a Guest Bath.* ABOVE RIGHT: *A painted Turkish sultana adds an exotic presence to the Master Bedroom.*

*The Russian secrétaire in the Master Bedroom displays
Greek and Etruscan vases. To the left is a French Directoire
chair. The 19th-century painting above is French.*

EIGHTEENTH-CENTURY AURA

Before arriving in Paris as the Spanish cultural attaché, Luis Sagrera held similar diplomatic posts in New Delhi and at The Hague. In each of these great cities he took pains to familiarize himself with the art of the countries involved. For he considers that his role as diplomat consists not only in representing his nation abroad but in absorbing the culture of foreign countries as well, and understanding those elements that bind all peoples. At an early age, in Madrid, the city where his family lives, Señor Sagrera developed his taste for paintings and fine antiques; later he began to concentrate on the art and history of those European countries where his diplomatic career took him. He was particularly fascinated with the eighteenth century. "At that time there was a Common Market of good taste and manners," he explains. And that century—with its elaborate court life and the magnificence of its kings—does seem like a golden age of culture and elegance.

His residence in Paris provided him the opportunity to gather together the objects acquired on his diplomatic travels. Few other houses in Paris could have afforded the appropriate background for his nostalgic evocation of the eighteenth century as does the townhouse in which his apartment is located. It stands on the Right Bank of the Seine, in an area where bankers and financiers have duplicated the charms of the Faubourg Saint-Germain, on the other side of the river. Even empty, the apartment was perfectly suited to Señor Sagrera's tastes. Nothing of an architectural nature was lacking, and there were lovely boiserie and mirrors and antique mantels. In order to move in, it was only necessary for the diplomat to place his own eighteenth-century furniture, put up paintings and drawings and arrange antique objects here and there on small tables. "Within three days," he says,

"I was completely at home." And there is an instant feeling that Señor Sagrera has *always* lived here. His knowledge of history and his passion for collecting have allowed him to re-create a décor from the past while giving the very real impression that this could well be the lodging of some Spanish diplomat at the court of Louis XV or Louis XVI.

However, the apartment is by no means rigid with eighteenth-century formality, although Luis Sagrera's important collections of architectural designs and drawings of galas and fêtes do suggest the glitter and grandeur of that century. "The eighteenth century," explains the Spanish diplomat, "was an era quite as luxurious and optimistic as our own seems skeptical and gloomy." But his desire has been less to raise philosophical issues than to make an intelligent reconstruction and to create a sense of era. Objects, for example, are not displayed for their ornamental value alone, but more for their ability to invoke a vanished time. The beautifully bound books with coats of arms upon them, the magnificent china from the Compagnie des Indes, the decorated boxes—all are valuable historical documents as well as being beautiful objects in themselves.

In a final demonstration of discipline, Luis Sagrera has resisted one of the great vices of the collector, the impulse to accumulate simply for the sake of accumulation. He has, in fact, stored away many of his possessions and prefers to replace an object with another of superior quality rather than indulge in a multiplication alone. So his gathering together of the past is warm and charming and civilized, and there is about his apartment a feeling of openness and even of informality. For Luis Sagrera is a diplomat as well as a collector, and his inclination makes it inevitable that his treasures will be shared with dignity by friends and colleagues alike.

In his Paris townhouse, Spanish diplomat Luis Sagrera evokes 18th-century refinement with a distinguished collection of art and antiques. The Salon pays homage to the Age of Reason. PRECEDING PAGE: Cantonese covered vases and Chinese Export plates add an Oriental aesthetic to the European opulence of a gilded Régence mirror and a Baroque Spanish console. LEFT: A pair of studies for a fresco are by Giaquinto; the floral composition is by Arellano, and the painting of Diana's bath is by van der Lisse. ABOVE: Over a Régence commode, a painting of ruins by Pannini is the center for an ensemble of artworks. At left are van Loo's portrait of Louis XV and a painting of Aeneas and Anchises; at right, a portrait of the duc d'Orleans, attributed to Pierre Mignard, and a view of Naples by Houel.

35

The sense of harmonious elegance continues in the Library. RIGHT: *A colorful Chinese wall-hanging serves as a naturalistic background for the classicism of an 18th-century architectural* modello. BELOW RIGHT: *The juxtaposition of 18th-century bronze emperor busts and a painting of Apollo and the Muses reflects the importance of historical and mythological subjects in the art of that century. The Charles IV desk couples geometric and floral marquetry.*

A diverse grouping of paintings, antique drawings and objects creates an inviting atmosphere in a corner of the Library. A 19th-century portrait and a historical scene of the Spanish court, both by Esquivel, and a floral study by Bartolomé Perez dominate the setting. A blazing fire illuminates the serene nymphs of a Directoire mantel, which bears a Louis XVI clock, small 19th-century figural sculptures of bronze, and gilded bronze Louis XVI candlesticks.

A SPECIAL FLAIR

With the first step into the expansive marble-floored entrance gallery of the Lewis Manilows' Chicago apartment, the sense of surprise and festivity that runs throughout the home boldly announces itself. The introductory space—like the many rooms beyond—is expectant and exuberant. The art is riveting, with its large scale, bold colors and imaginative subject matter. The architectural background is quite another matter. From the marble floor to the gracefully carved Art Déco overdoors and classic detailing of woodwork and cornices, it is clear that this was once a most traditional apartment in the grand style of the 1920s.

The interior was originally built for another collector, Chauncey McCormick, who, at one time, was president of the Art Institute of Chicago. Mr. Manilow is the former president of Chicago's Museum of Contemporary Art, and the apartment now mirrors his forward-looking taste and extensive knowledge of art. Were Mr. McCormick to re-enter his former residence and be confronted by a huge Photo-Realist painting of three youths flanked by the head and hand of a dismembered giant—in reality, a Robert Arneson bust of himself, and a Pedro Friedeberg "hand" chair—he might well be startled. But he would be gratified by the careful preservation of the interior architecture, which the Manilows entrusted to a friend, Chicago interior designer Bruce Gregga.

The Manilow collections range from antique Turkish rugs to Mannerist engravings to Chicago Funk Art—with excursions into Surrealism, Abstract Expressionism and Pop Art. In this diversity, the unifying factor that runs throughout, with the exception of the Turkish rugs and the few abstract paintings, is a strongly mannered vision of figuration, which appears again and again. These images are represented in the Manilow collection by artists as otherwise unrelated as Dürer, Goltzius, Balthus, Georgia O'Keeffe, Richard Lindner and H. C. Westermann. To house such a collection in an essentially staid eighteenth-century-inspired interior is in itself a mannerism. But in every room the total success of the delicate operation is reconfirmed. Colors range from white to natural oak, from off-white to dark gray, which Mr. and Mrs. Manilow find "provide a wonderful ground where everything shows to maximum advantage." Although furnishings are kept at a minimum, what furniture there is tends to be exceptional: a Spanish coffer, a low table made from an ancient Syrian mosaic, superb Queen Anne dining room chairs—a bit of everything. "But the Manilows don't have something from every period simply to be chic," Bruce Gregga explains. "They have a very personal attitude to living and collecting. The eclectic is something they appreciate."

How have the Manilows collected? They have been guided by gradual shifts in-taste and by new discoveries—aided by accidents. "There have been many marvelous accidents," they recall. "We went to Parke-Bernet to look for Mannerist prints, and bought the dining room chairs. As for the Mannerist prints, the first ones we bought were themselves added to the collection by accident. We were in Los Angeles, walking down La Cienega Boulevard, and saw a Goltzius in a window." The apartment is, as Mr. Manilow observes, a home and not a gallery, and the highly original collections are reflections of the residents' wit and imagination. There are all the elements of eminently congenial and hospitable surroundings put together with a high level of enthusiasm. Art and people are at home, but it is primarily a residence where Mr. and Mrs. Lewis Manilow have, in their words, "a wonderful time."

PRECEDING PAGE: *The Entrance Gallery of Mr. and Mrs. Lewis Manilow's Chicago apartment recalls classic formality while showcasing modern artworks. Paintings are by Ed Paschke and Franz Gertsch; sculptures, from left, by H.C. Westermann, Robert Arneson, Pedro Friedeberg and Claes Oldenburg.* LEFT: *French-inspired paneling in the Living Room provides a neutral foil for the artworks: from left, a Richard Lindner drawing, a Balthus portrait and two Mannerist prints. Figures on the mantel are by Degas and Etrog; below the Lindner drawing is a sculpture by Mark di Suvero; at left is an Indonesian bird carving.* BELOW: *The ancient Syrian mosaic tabletop in the Living Room contrasts with contemporary art. Bold paintings are by Richard Lindner and Mark Rothko. The sculpture on the pedestal is by Richard Hunt;* Inverted Q, *on the piano, is by Claes Oldenburg.*

The simply furnished Dining Room is distinguished by the residents' fine collection of Turkish rugs: a 17th-century prayer rug from Transylvania adorns one wall; the 18th-century rug on the floor is from Smyrna. Queen Anne chairs are upholstered in 19th-century needlepoint.

Dining Room walls upholstered in dark suedelike fabric set off rugs mounted as works of art. At center is a 17th-century rug from the Ottoman court. English candlesticks are displayed on the 18th-century Italian refectory table. The contemporary sculpture is by John Henry.

OPPOSITE ABOVE LEFT: *In the paneled Library, an atypical Jean Dubuffet gouache surmounts a culturally varied grouping consisting of, from left, a Robert Arneson bust, an American Indian bowl, a Reuben Nakian sculpture, two Nigerian sculptures and a cycladic idol.* OPPOSITE ABOVE RIGHT: *Claes Oldenburg's* Eraser *adds a note of whimsy in the Library.* OPPOSITE: *Another Dubuffet painting provides a focal point in the Library; on the table is a Germaine Richier sculpture. Gothic-style Windsor chairs and a Turkish rug complete the setting.* ABOVE: *A Frank Stella canvas dominates the Master Bedroom. The bedcovering was inspired by a Morris Louis painting.*

A HERITAGE OF TASTE

"What started me as a collector was living with beautiful things. My father was a collector, too," relates Whitney Warren. His home on San Francisco's Telegraph Hill is practically a historic landmark of interior design, built by the renowned architect Gardner Dailey, decorated originally by Billy Baldwin and later refurbished by Anthony Hail.

Mr. Warren acquired the four mirrored panels in the hall, formerly doors in a palace in Genoa, at auction in New York. "They once belonged to Mr. and Mrs. Guest, who had used them as a screen. I decided I wanted them after learning that they had also belonged to Stanford White, the great architect for whom my father worked in his first job. That made it doubly interesting for me. The panels were brought to California, and they fitted exactly. It was fantastic." Whitney Warren, Sr., who died in 1943, was the architect for Grand Central Station and for the reconstruction (1928) of the University of Louvain, in Belgium, destroyed during World War I. He also designed the John Paul Jones crypt at the U.S. Naval Academy, the bronze gates of the Cathedral of St. John the Divine, in New York, and the Belmont and Ritz-Carlton hotels.

The heritage of good taste he bequeathed to his son is immediately evident in the entrance hall, where the mirrored panels reflect potted trees and an eighteenth-century Venetian chandelier illuminates the alcove formed by the balcony. One high wall displays a Flemish tapestry with a coat of arms. "It's not my world at all, but it's very good," says Mr. Warren. On the opposite wall, over the stairs, the eighteenth-century French verdure tapestries are "hung properly. Instead of being stretched out, they're hung like tapestries in France, softly draped." The hall opens to the living room, where a nineteen-foot ceiling is punctuated by an eighteenth-century

chandelier made in Venice and reworked by the English. On each side of the hearth stands a Venetian glass lantern, "either from a church, or else they are what the Venetians call *fanali,* great lighting things that were put in front of palaces." A large Russian table, formerly owned by the czars, had been taken to England before Mr. Warren acquired it in Rome. "It had perfectly awful legs, which I had removed; the Romans made new legs for it."

Between the living room and the library stretches a loggia, and beyond it a stunning view of the city. Directly ahead, towering over the rooftops, loom the Transamerica pyramid and the Bank of America building. To the left, Mr. Warren's prospect includes San Francisco Bay and the Bay Bridge. On the floor above, the master bedroom opens onto the same vista. The austere steel bed belonged to one of Napoleon's advisors, Cambacérès, from whose descendants it was acquired. Over the bed is an early Boldini, and nearby are an oil sketch by the same artist of his *Duchess of Marlborough,* a Drian painting of Mr. Warren's mother and several Stuempfigs, "who I think will come to be appreciated as one of the very great American artists in years to come."

About his selection of paintings, tapestries and furniture, Mr. Warren says, "I buy anything I can afford that I like. But I haven't got any more room." Would he give up some of his possessions to make room for more? No, indeed. "I'd hang them in the garage," he laughs. This connoisseur's taste extends to a bit of whimsy on occasion, such as the two Chinese figures of pandas he picked up on a trip to Japan and placed in the hall amid his European treasures. They are effective because the level of taste prevails. "It makes a good house," Whitney Warren concludes of his collection and its place in his home, "an intelligent house for a bachelor to live in."

PRECEDING PAGE: *In Whitney Warren's San Francisco home, an 18th-century Venetian chandelier illuminates the Entrance Hall. French tapestries softly drape the stairwell.*
LEFT: *Louis XV chairs and a Louis XVI painted marble-topped table in the Entrance Hall are backdropped by four mirrored 18th-century palace doors.* OPPOSITE: *An antique wooden surround defines the Drawing Room doorway. The ornamental architectural painting is Italian. A Russian lapis-topped table holds a Chinese figural sculpture and an 18th-century French revolving clock.* FOLLOWING PAGES: *In the Drawing Room, an 18th-century Venetian mirror is displayed in front of a Louis XV trumeau and mantel. A Venetian glass lantern stands beside the fireplace. The Italian architectural paintings are early 17th century, and the four framed tile scenes are from drawings by Tiepolo.*

OPPOSITE: *Houdon's marble bust of a French nobleman enriches the Drawing Room. The hardstone mosaic-topped table holds an urn of lapis with bronze mounts, a classical marble head and porphyry, gilt-bronze-mounted vessels.*

ABOVE: *A portrait of Mr. Warren's mother, by Boldini, contributes a graceful presence to the Library. The Louis XV marquetry commode displays an 18th-century leather clock by Berthoud. The chairs and bureau plat are also Louis XV.* RIGHT: *Formerly in the collection of Prince Talleyrand, an 18th-century porcelain figure represents one of the four Moors sculpted by Pietro Tacca for the monument to Ferdinando Medici, in Leghorn.*

OLD BATTERSEA HOUSE

Across the Thames from London, sandwiched between the edges of the river and modern apartment blocks, stands a graceful seventeenth-century house. It is *Old Battersea House*, attributed to the great English architect Sir Christopher Wren and carefully restored by its present tenant, the American publisher Malcolm Forbes, in 1970. Mr. Forbes is a passionate collector—houses definitely included. In addition to this residence, there are ranches in Montana and Wyoming, an estate in New Jersey, a palace in Tangier, a château near Deauville, and more.

Old Battersea House was built in 1699, probably on the site of a Tudor dwelling. There is the story that at one time in its history the house was owned by a sea captain, who would jump into his boat and head upstream whenever he had to do business in London. In the nineteenth century the home became a school for young ladies and later was leased to a Colonel and Mrs. Stirling. After her husband's death, Mrs. Stirling stayed on. She was the sister of the Pre-Raphaelite painter Evelyn de Morgan, and the house was used as a museum to show both her sister's work and that of her brother-in-law, William de Morgan. At present the de Morgan Collection, which has been exhibited in the United States, is in storage in London. It is hoped that, in the not too distant future, it will be returned to Old Battersea House and put on display there once again.

Meanwhile, the house continues to accommodate some of the precious items of the Forbeses' collections. Most dominant is the group of Victorian paintings, which appear in almost every corner of the residence—including the vast kitchen, where a painting of enormous proportions surmounts the pine table. There are Alma-Tadema maidens, barefooted, tambourined and flower-wreathed, framed along the stairs; bright-eyed Landseer dogs in the bedroom; Queen Victoria, young and crinolined, in various rooms, and reposing sheep in the hall. Mythical scenes, tearful departures, weddings in white and scenes of knighthood are elsewhere. The collections exhibited at Old Battersea House are truly eclectic. Victorian masterpieces may monopolize the walls, but precious statuary is at the foot of the stairs, cheek by jowl with machines from a motorbike collection, and in a room with a double fireplace there rests an entire flotilla of model boats.

When Mr. Forbes took over the house, the rebuilding operation was given over to architect Vernon Gibbard. His work included demolishing the Victorian wing of the house to restore the purity of its original lines. Floorboards were imported from Russia to replace age-worn ones, since Mr. Gibbard maintains it is impossible to get hold of sufficiently wide planks in Britain. The garden was landscaped by Vernon Russell-Smith, and the decoration for two of the rooms on the ground floor was done entirely by interior designer Elizabeth Winn. "Mr. Forbes wanted a large area of grass, and privacy," says Mr. Russell-Smith. "In order to give that privacy, we removed loads of dreary London privet and overgrown laurel and put up a raised trellis with bamboo and *Mahonias*. We added a yew hedge and old-fashioned roses to create a very English look."

Mr. Forbes is pleased with the result of the restoration: "I call it a bringing together, rather than a decorating project. The excitement about collecting is that, wherever you go, you're kept on the alert. Because we always go to auctions, we're stimulated to look out for new things. And that's what makes our collections so diverse." And his favorite collection? "Probably the Fabergé. No, collections don't give me a feeling of great responsibility—no doubt because, above all, they're a *passion* with me."

Publisher Malcolm Forbes has restored Old Battersea House, an early-Georgian residence in London, as a setting for his collection of English furniture and paintings. PRECEDING PAGE: In the Garden Room, an 1867 portrait of Queen Victoria, by J. H. Thompson, is accompanied by a small Charles Lock Eastlake portrait and mythological subjects by William Dyce and William Etty. LEFT: Victorian artworks in the Sitting Room include William Powell Frith's anecdotal 1881 canvas, For Better, For Worse, above the fireplace; Sir William Q. Orchardson's **The** Queen of the Swords, at left; and, above the doorway, H. N. O'Neil's replication of sensitive details from two of his narrative works. ABOVE: A corner of the Sitting Room features J. J. Tissot's 'Good Bye'—On the Mersey.

RIGHT: *A portrait by William Holman Hunt, in the Sitting Room, combines the characteristics of two women the artist loved.* BELOW RIGHT: *An 1869 work by Robert Scott Lauder spans a Guest Room wall. Chintz wallcovering reinterprets a 19th-century design.* OPPOSITE: *Sir Edward J. Poynter's* The Prodigal's Return, *which enjoyed great critical success in 1869, dominates the Master Bedroom. At left is George F. Watts's 1869 oil,* Orpheus and Eurydice, *accompanied by a mezzotint of it by Frank Short.*

HOMAGE TO RODIN

The word generosity has many definitions—and B. Gerald Cantor could well be one of them. Possibly the world's greatest collector of Rodin sculpture, he has, over the past several years, made a series of donations that are considered the most important gifts of sculpture, and the most valuable, ever made in the United States. Yet a visit to Mr. and Mrs. Cantor's New York apartment hardly betrays the loss. In fact, the array of Rodin bronzes is so dazzling it is at first difficult to realize that this is a private residence and not the wing of some great museum. Undeniably, however, there is no "museum" feeling here. In part, this is achieved by the extremely simple but rich furnishings created by New York interior designer Bebe Winkler. Of all the arts, sculpture is perhaps the most difficult to live with because it needs not only actual space but visual space as well. It cannot be read properly if it is not seen in the round, and this concept had to be taken into consideration in organizing the décor of the apartment. The result achieved by Miss Winkler provides a background that complements the art while maintaining a real strength of its own.

Having spent over thirty years assembling the largest and most comprehensive private collection of an artist generally considered to be the greatest sculptor of the nineteenth century, Mr. Cantor clearly must be in awe of Auguste Rodin. Such a feeling, however, is in no way apparent. Mr. Cantor views his sculpture collection with modesty and deference, as though he were only a caretaker for objects that belong to no one man but to the world. To acquire such a comprehensive collection is a remarkable feat in an era when corporations and museums and individuals are competing fiercely for a dwindling supply of masterpieces. Mr. Cantor was helped considerably by a fact that not many people knew at the time he started collecting: The Musée Rodin in Paris had in its vast storerooms hundreds of works by the sculptor—studies and models in plaster, as well as pieces considered finished but never cast in Rodin's lifetime. Under the imaginative direction of Mme Goldscheider, the museum began casting pieces in small limited editions. Considering the magnitude of the project, it took a collector of genuine discernment to select the most important and seminal works. Mr. Cantor was that man.

A visit to the apartment reveals Mr. Cantor's interest in other sculptors, as well as in painters. For instance, he has been collecting the work of Georg Kolbe since 1960, and he is said to have the largest collection of Kolbe's sculpture outside of Germany. Of all the paintings in the Cantor collection, perhaps the one that leaves the most lasting impression is the 1918 Vlaminck portrait of the poet Fritz Vanderpyl. This well-known landscape artist here reveals himself as a portrait painter of rare insight and intensity. There is also an Oskar Kokoschka portrait of an Italian peasant woman, dated 1933. In Mr. Cantor's study there is a remarkable group of paintings—among them the Pissarro *Le Marché*, of 1833; a Eugene Carrière, *La Nouvelle Montre-Bracelet*; a Signac of 1909, *Le Jardin à Saint-Tropez*. The living room has a magnificent *Eve* by Roger de la Fresnaye; a Robert Delaunay of 1904; a Kandinsky; and a Sisley, *Le Marronnier à Saint-Mammès*. The dining room contains not only a fine Henri Martin pointillist landscape but two of Rodin's most famous works as well: a study for the Balzac monument and a study for *Eve*. His Manhattan apartment reveals Mr. Cantor and his stature as a collector. He is certainly a man who knows how to give grandly but who prefers to live, like a true Maecenas, surrounded by great art in a noble and harmonious setting.

Designer Bebe Winkler transformed
the Manhattan home of Mr. and Mrs.
B. Gerald Cantor into an understated
setting for their collection of Rodin sculptures. PRECEDING PAGE: *A mirrored wall
between the Living Room and the Entrance Hall reflects an assemblage of
smaller Rodin bronzes.* RIGHT: *Works
by others set the sculptor in perspective,
as in the Entrance Area, where Rodin's
Adam coexists with a female figure by
Georg Kolbe and a painting by the Russian modernist Mikhail Larionov.* BELOW
RIGHT: *As a group of small studies reveals,
Rodin devoted special attention to the
expressiveness of the human hand.*

62

In the Living Room, Rodin's The Thinker *overlooks a collection of smaller pieces by the sculptor. On the wall are a landscape by Sisley and smaller canvases by Utrillo, left, and Kandinsky, right.*

63

ABOVE: *Large pieces in the Living Room include Roger de la Fresnaye's* Eve *and a figural sculpture by Kolbe. On one table is a trio of small Rodin dancers; on the other, Rodin's* Large Left Hand with Despairing Adolescent.

The muted color scheme is deepened somewhat in the Dining Room, where a porcelain vase filled with irises lends aesthetic delicacy to the dining table. The mirrored niche is filled with the robust energy of Rodin's Naked Balzac.

OPPOSITE: *Maurice de Vlaminck's brooding portrait of poet
Fritz Vanderpyl dominates a corner of the Library. On the
low table rests a small Rodin sculpture.* ABOVE: *Jean Louis
Forain's painting* Femme à sa toilette *and a graceful
portrait by Giovanni Boldini complement an ensemble of
small Rodin bronzes in the Master Bedroom. The canopy
bed, striped with silk taffeta, injects linear refinement.*
RIGHT: *The original plaster of Rodin's* Hand of God *reveals the Mannerist complexity of the sculptor's art.*

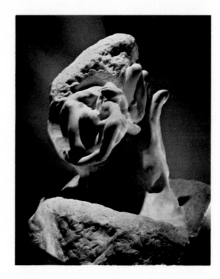

OLD WORLD SIMPLICITY

Fred Wehmer's apartment in New York City is in quintessential Greenwich Village. Here are the familiar ailanthus trees lining narrow, patched sidewalks. Here too are the old buildings that make Village streets a living history book of urban American architecture. Altogether it is an aged neighborhood, surviving with success. The house in which Mr. Wehmer's apartment is located was built in 1836 and fits handsomely into this scene. But walk through that door and enter Mr. Wehmer's inner sanctum, and another world awaits—one that looks more like Vienna in the 1830s than present-day New York. For Fred Wehmer fancies Biedermeier furniture—Germany's version of Neo-Classicism —and he has created living and working quarters for himself that are serene, witty and comfortable.

How did Fred Wehmer, a painter by vocation, become a captive to this arcane, pre-Victorian style? "When I came to New York to study at the Art Students League, I had very few possessions and happened upon a Biedermeier chair in a shop, and I bought it. Most dealers then didn't really value the style and made no particular fuss over it. The next thing I knew, I stumbled upon a table, and bought that. Some months later I found a Biedermeier mirror to hang over the table—and I was hooked!"

From the start he was attracted to both the physical appearance of the furniture—"In its purity of line, color and shape it fits my personal vision"— and the simple life that nurtured it. Mr. Wehmer speaks knowledgeably about the history of the period: "The style, in its purest form, lasted scarcely fifteen years, from 1816 to 1830. Then it began to go in the direction of Victorian overelaboration and heaviness. Biedermeier was designed by middle-class craftsmen for middle-class people who cared more about their comfort than they did about show.

The Germans and Austrians, by the way, had taken a hard economic beating during the Napoleonic Wars, and they were in no mood for the kind of flamboyance that the English gentry were exhibiting. Biedermeier furniture is almost chaste in its ornament, and its decoration often comes from the wood itself. The pieces are very two-dimensional, designed to be seen frontally. It takes its name from a cartoon character, 'Papa Biedermeier,' who was to the next generation of Germans a rather lovable symbol of everything bourgeois and reactionary. The name, I suppose, was meant as a reproach."

The collection fits into two rooms and an assortment of alcoves that occupy what must have been the parlor floor of the building. Though Germany is far from New York, furniture and interior architectural details harmonize. "It's not really coincidence. This house and that cupboard," he says, indicating a nearly six-foot-high piece, "are contemporaries. Both were built in the 1830s to suit middle-class life. The proportions are right, and if you look at the rather angular architectural lines of the fireplace and the lines of the cupboard, you can see they are very close in feeling." He is understandably delighted that his house and his furniture are so compatible, but he is quick to say that he is no antiquarian bent on re-creating someone else's reality. And he is not intimidated by the value of his collection.

As for such features of the apartment as window treatments, upholstery fabrics, rugs and the color scheme, Fred Wehmer has a relaxed attitude: "If it works, it works. Mama and Papa Biedermeier would undoubtedly have preferred something more elaborate than the matchstick blinds I've used, but for me the richness of the furniture is most certainly enough." He would wholeheartedly endorse Mies van der Rohe's famous dictum: "Less is more."

The simplicity of a Greenwich Village apartment provides
a serene atmosphere for Fred Wehmer's extensive collection
of Biedermeier furniture. PRECEDING PAGE: In the Sitting
Room, the temperate lines of the settee and tables exemplify
the Neo-Classic style that was popular in Germany from
1816 to 1830. French park chairs further the spare appeal
of the room. LEFT AND ABOVE: Other Biedermeier pieces—
including a large table, dining chairs, a chest and a cupboard designed to look like a secrétaire—occupy the Sitting
Room. Arranged around the Empire temple clock are Greek
and Roman gemstone seals and Etruscanware plates. Mr.
Wehmer's own paintings adorn the walls.

OPPOSITE: *A blazing hearth in the Studio adds a cheery glow to the distinctive, warm-toned Biedermeier veneers. The lines of the table, chairs and daybed contribute grace to the versatile room, used for dining and sleeping as well as painting. The chandelier is a 1920s version of French Directoire.* LEFT: *A Biedermeier vitrine holds a collection of objects, including tea caddies and snuff boxes of both tortoiseshell and faux-tortoiseshell; objects in ivory, jade and horn; and Roman glass.*

CONTEMPORARY ELAN

Art plays an ambiguous role in many interiors. All too often it is placed in a room with little or no regard for the demands of the space. Conversely, it is often situated in such a way that it totally overwhelms the setting, managing, by overlighting or maladroit scale, to intimidate and confuse. The question of how to place art properly in an environment, however, has been intelligently answered by Betty Lee Stern in her house in Beverly Hills. With her husband, Dr. Aaron Stern, as an enthusiastic supporter, she organized their house—designed in 1952 by Maurice Fleishman—into a coherent setting for works by southern California artists.

"Please don't call me a collector," says Mrs. Stern, with a note of humorous irony. "It would make everything I do seem self-conscious and affected, whereas everything you see in this house is really a very simple response. A response to California—I grew up in New England—the hedonistic light, the climate. It is a response to the art I found here and, eastern skeptics to the contrary, this part of the world has produced some extraordinarily powerful and mature works. Finally, it is a response to a deep-seated need I have to make art explicable. Many people are intimidated by contemporary art, and often this is because they see it in museums and galleries. In this house, I attempted to show it in the context of living spaces—to introduce it against a background of animation and laughter, rather than in the silence of some public institution."

The context of these private views is serene. Light-toned walls, terrazzo floors, carefully controlled lighting and a harmonious sense of scale are all qualities that are invoked by Mrs. Stern's remodeling, accomplished with the help of interior designer Jack Brogan. Perhaps even more important is the vivid relationship the house enjoys with its surroundings. Everywhere the art is seen in the context of views; paintings become commentaries on nature and statues open dialogues with the complex forms of trees and vegetation. The rooms are in a sense minimalist, yet they are rich in one of southern California's more tangible assets—light.

Another aspect of the house makes it a particularly appropriate setting for modern art—simple function. Although it is a luxurious shell—the gleaming walls and pristine floors radiate the glow of fine materials—nothing in it is difficult to maintain. Making art a part of everyday experience is an impulse that can easily lead to a rather academic display of erudition. But there is nothing distant about Mrs. Stern. She explains the motives behind her unique synthesis of disciplines with modesty: "I really know very little about art. I never set out to produce a tour de force or make a great original statement. I was simply moved by certain things and wanted to make them part of my life."

As a result of her involvement with the artists shown in the house, friends began to ask her for advice, artists came to her for information about potential buyers and, in an almost accidental way, she found herself developing a vocation. "I find people very perceptive in California," she remarks. Leaning over the sofa table, she balances a glass of water on a wooden box. "You see, in California someone would look at this and say, 'Great, it's new, we love it!' I'm not being disparaging; I think it's wonderfully healthy. Aaron and I are planning to return to the East Coast, and I'm wondering if I'll find the same degree of receptivity to my ideas." Whatever Mrs. Stern chooses to do, one thing is certain. The civilized eye and talent for placement will go with her, ensuring the same degree of delight wherever she chooses to locate her collection.

Champions of southern California art, Betty Lee Stern and
her husband, Dr. Aaron Stern, remodeled their Beverly
Hills home to create a complementary environment for a
highly contemporary collection. PRECEDING PAGE: In the Living Room, Robert Graham's bronze, Lise II, is a lithe coun-
terpart to John McCracken's monolithic resin sculpture.
ABOVE: A Sam Francis canvas provides an arresting focus
at one end of the Living Room. The translucent polyester
sculpture on the marble table is by Terrence O'Shea.

Color and form, contained and uncontained, are preoccupations in the Ronald Davis painting titled Dual Hexagon Radials #512, *spanning another Living Room wall.*

RIGHT: *The cloudlike forms of Joe Goode's* Malibu *create a striking background for the Robert Graham sculpture in the Living Room. A contoured wall gradually curves toward a bold John McLaughlin painting.*

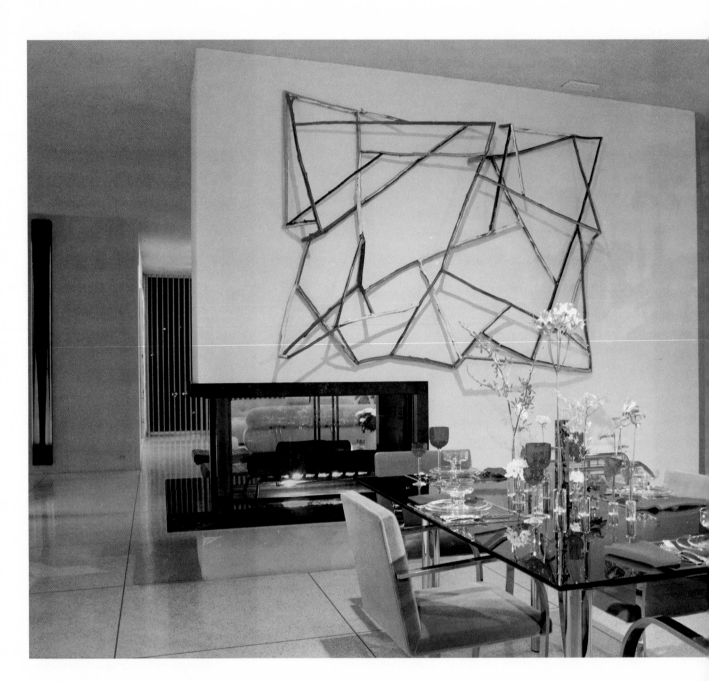

*A Charles Arnoldi tree-branch wall
sculpture brightens the Dining Room.
Mies van der Rohe chairs surround the
glass-topped table. The terrazzo floor
and a double fireplace of chrome, glass
and marble add lustrous highlights.*

ABOVE RIGHT: *In the Den, geometrics prevail in Ronald Davis's* Open Slab in Vent #472, *John McLaughlin's* Painting #11 *and John McCracken's dark resin sculpture.* RIGHT: *Robert Graham's bronze torso and Ronald Davis's* Square Wave Duct #544 *enliven the Study. Bookshelves separate the study from the master bedroom.*

*A pair of collage paintings by Don Sorenson add dyna-
mism to the austere Master Bedroom; Gwynn Murrill's
wooden cat stretches indolently. Charles Arnoldi's oval
painting rests in a setting of built-in shelves.*

John McLaughlin's stark Black and White #10 *continues the minimal theme of the Master Bedroom. The dark marble raised hearth of the fireplace and pale vertical blinds echo the refrain, as does the dark fringe of a wool rug.*

83

A FORMAL SALON

When art historian and lecturer Robert Allen streamlined his environment to allow himself more freedom to travel for both work and pleasure, he surrendered none of his most precious possessions—his books, his works of art or his collection of fine furniture. He gave up an extensive duplex apartment at the Hotel des Artistes in Manhattan for a studio apartment in the Murray Hill neighborhood. A magnificent room entirely paneled in solid cherry, it was once the back parlor of a house designed by Stanford White and built by J. P. Morgan as a present for one of his daughters. There is little else to the apartment but an efficiency kitchen, a bath and a dressing alcove. But it has become the perfect setting for the appointments Mr. Allen refuses to do without. "Not one chair was disposed of," he says, and the apartment has over twelve of them.

Possessions are placed so as to be enjoyed leisurely. Black velvet and lacquered table surfaces, chests and a *bureau plat* offset the brilliant tapestried furniture. A lacquered screen is the focal point of the room, giving emphasis to entrances and exits. All of the seating is French and mainly Art Déco, with the exception of one eighteenth-century Venetian chair and two Régence fauteuils. The drama of the room is provided by the gilt canapé and suite of bergères and fauteuils by Süe et Mare covered in Beauvais tapestry by Bénédictus. They were prominent attractions at the Exposition des Arts Décoratifs in Paris in 1925. Opposite is a cozy grouping of a velvet upholstered settee and armchairs, and an arrangement of black-lacquered Japanese tea tables. Antique kilim rugs casually cover the floors, and there are cushions of nineteenth-century Chinese tribute silk, all arranged invitingly on the divan.

Standing sentinel in the corners of the room are grand torchères in silver and bronze, created by architect John Barrington Bayley, who designed the new wing of the Frick Museum. Picture lights and pale nineteenth-century celadon vases made into lamps are the only other sources of illumination in the room, except for candles in eighteenth-century Wedgwood Titans, ritually lit at the dinner hour. The solid, beautifully made Louis XV-style *bureau plat* serves as a desk and worktable, and steel and brass gueridons designed by John Vesey hold precious bibelots. Abundant arrangements of peonies, irises and baby's breath are always present in handsome Lalique vases of classic proportions.

On the walls are the unusual paintings that only an art historian, with an eye that discerns quality rather than fashionable taste, would collect. There is a rare Pierre Subleyras of the 1720s, *The Release of Prometheus by Hercules*, which until its discovery a few years ago was known only from a self-portrait of the artist in his own studio; a *Baptism of Christ* by Francesco Albani of Bologna resting nonchalantly on a window sill in its eighteenth-century carved frame; and a Francesco Gessi, a collaborator of Guido Reni in the 1630s, representing a still life that adds a sharp, surreal note. Dominating the room from its place over the chimneypiece is a work by Theodor van Thulden, an artist from the circle of Rubens, and facing it is a melodramatic nineteenth-century Symbolist vision of a graveyard by the side of a roaring sea. Works by Dulac, Descamps and Benjamin Constant have their niches, as well as modern works by Steven Kuzma and Ed Armour. It is not easy to discover where Mr. Allen, in this miniature setting, manages to find room for his clothes and other personal possessions. That, however, is his secret—the same secret that makes it possible for him to produce a superb *boeuf à la mode en gelée* or a *blanquette de veau* in his lilliputian kitchen.

Moving from a large duplex apartment to a studio suite in Manhattan, art historian Robert Allen sacrificed none of his cherished possessions. PRECEDING PAGE: *Two tapestried Régence chairs appoint the fireside. The painting is by Theodor van Thulden.* RIGHT: *A gilt canapé and suite of chairs by Süe et Mare, upholstered in Beauvais tapestry designed by Bénédictus, harmonize in Art Déco splendor with velvet-covered pieces of the same period. A Lalique vase and two Burmese bowls rest on the lacquered table at the right. Large paintings, from left to right, are by Francesco Albani, Francesco Gessi and Adolf Hirémy-Hirschl. The small watercolor is by Descamps.*

Artworks in the Living Area include a
large 18th-century painting by Pierre
Subleyras; on the table, a 1912 watercolor by Edmund Dulac; and, near the
window, a contemporary painting by
Stephen Kuzma. The bust is by Jean-
Jacques Caffieri. At left is a group
of 18th-century crystal decanters.

A brilliantly colored Art Déco screen,
circa 1925, dramatizes an intimate
seating group in the Living Area.
Behind the screen are bookcases finished
in lacquer and gold leaf, with shelves
covered in leather. Above the coroman-
del cabinet in the corner is a 1976
abstract painting by Edward Armour.

THE REFINEMENTS OF ART DECO

In those brief years between the end of World War I and the Great Depression, the decorative arts in France enjoyed their last fling. Artists indulged themselves with rich materials coupled not only with the superb craftsmanship that had distinguished the eighteenth century, but also with a purity of form and line that edited out the frivolous ornamentations of the nineteenth century. When the great exposition of these styles opened in 1925 in Paris, it set standards of excellence in design for the twentieth century. "Art Déco," as this style has come to be called, had an urbanity and a suaveness that have had no equal since. It is the splendor of this period that speaks in the Manhattan apartment of art gallery owner Andrew Crispo.

"I like the simplicity of Art Déco and the way it relates to painting of the same era, even to American painting," says Mr. Crispo. "My interest in American art is clearly in the artists of that period—Arthur Dove, Georgia O'Keeffe, Stuart Davis, William Zorach. I also consider the great furniture makers of the time artists, and I respond to their understanding of proportion and design as well as to their feeling for craftsmanship and materials of quality." Andrew Crispo hastens to point out that the term "Art Déco" unfortunately has come to include countless objects representing the lowest common denominator of the period's popular taste. It was, after all, an era when a much-publicized café society discovered that jazz was hot, the generation was lost, and the martini had replaced morning coffee. They created objects absurdly disproportionate to their use, and decorated them with zigzags, flying wedges, chromed rods and plexiglass discs.

"There was a lot of bad work done in the Déco period," he observes. "Ten percent was really incredible, and the rest was just bad design." Mr. Crispo's living/dining room is dominated by notes of superb quality: furniture by Frank and Ruhlmann; statues by Archipenko and the Martels; paintings by Dove, O'Keeffe and Davis; and a scattering of ornamental objects by proto-Déco designer Josef Hoffmann. The pale-toned background of the room intensifies the pure contours of the furniture, and was created for Mr. Crispo by a friend, Arthur E. Smith, who also helped select the rare furnishings in the apartment.

Andrew Crispo's refined taste for collecting developed in a somewhat unusual fashion. As a boy in Philadelphia he found the galleries and collections of the city's museum of art a favorite refuge as well as a contrast to the life of the orphanage in which he was raised. "I usually went on Sunday afternoons," he recalls, "and always discovered new and wonderful things. When I came to New York at eighteen I went to work for an antiques dealer. I lived with furniture eight hours a day and spent my leisure time reading and doing research. Certainly New York itself had a lot to do with developing my taste. I began collecting right away." He is a true collector, and he believes that the real collector acquires anything he wants to acquire. "Maybe he can't afford it, but he manages. For myself, I've never been afraid to part with money for an object, and I'll even pay more than I know something is worth—simply because I really love it and want it." Although Andrew Crispo owns one of New York's leading galleries of modern art, he makes it an absolute rule never to sell anything bought for his own collection. "I don't even exchange in order to 'upgrade,' because there's no 'upgrading' to be done if you really love something. The collector should buy not because of fashion, but because of liking. There's no reason for my collections, beyond the fact that I really *like* these things."

*Works by leading artists, designers and craftsmen of the
1920s and 1930s distinguish collector Andrew Crispo's
Manhattan apartment, designed by Arthur E. Smith.*
PRECEDING PAGE: *The robust 1920s classicism of Emile
Jacques Ruhlmann armchairs dominates a corner of the
Living Room. The paintings are by Arthur Dove. The
1925 table, also by Ruhlmann, bears a Josef Hoffmann
brass vase, circa 1910.* ABOVE: *The Entrance Hall fea-
tures a 1933 William Zorach bronze sculpture and a 1919
Georgia O'Keeffe oil painting. Cork folding screens by the
Art Déco designer Eileen Gray direct the spatial flow.*

Morris Louis's 1958 painting Beth Feh *and a Bambara
sculpture preside over another Living Room arrangement.
A 1929 shagreen table by Jean-Michel Frank stands on
the 1925 Evelyn Wyld rug, which unifies the setting.*

ABOVE: *In the Living Room, a lustrous 1925 Jean-Michel
Frank desk holds a Lalique vase and a fluted brass cup,
1910–12, by Josef Hoffmann. At center is Archipenko's*
Flat Torso. OPPOSITE: *The Dining Area occupies one
corner of the living room. Here, a chrome-pedestaled table
is surrounded by Jean-Michel Frank chairs, 1929; the
place settings are composed of Art Déco flatware by Jean
Puiforcat and handpainted Tiffany plates. Artworks include a Stuart Davis painting,* Rue Lippe; *a terra-cotta
accordion player by Joël and Jan Martel; and two Georgia
O'Keeffe studies,* Black Diagonal *and* Black Lines.

In the Bedroom, more restricted tones and artworks from the 1970s vary the design emphasis. OPPOSITE: In Plato's Cave, *a 1973 canvas by Robert Motherwell, and* Black Spheres, *a 1976 wall sculpture by Varujan Boghosian, add dark poetry to the décor.* ABOVE: *A varied arrangement centers around a 1915 study by Marcel Duchamp, after his history-making* Nude Descending a Staircase. *A 1925 Wedgwood vase reiterates the taut color scheme of the room, while an Egyptian limestone bird and a tortoiseshell mirror frame provide earth-toned warmth. Arthur Dove's 1929 drawing* Whew *is seen in reflection.*

PRE-COLUMBIAN ART

In a certain respect, Caracas is reminiscent of Los Angeles. The city spreads over a steep range that rises a little inland from the ocean, to create a dramatic site, although in between—in the clefts and valleys—are the busy freeways and crowded neighborhoods of a capital steadily growing bigger in the approved modern style. In much of Caracas there is very little room for the sentimentalist. But certain outlying areas, like San Bernardino, offer fine views as well as homes with a sense of seclusion. Here the accent is on privacy and domesticity, on up-to-date design with comfort. The house of Harry and Maxula Mannil is no exception to this general rule.

The Mannils have more than domestic needs, however, for their home must cater to the collector's mania. All his life, Mr. Mannil explains, he has wanted to collect, but did not have the opportunity in his youth. Born in Estonia, he escaped in the middle of World War II to Scandinavia, then to Venezuela. At first he established himself in Maracaibo, where his wife, Maxula, comes from, and became chairman of what he calls "a small conglomerate." Since it is impossible to collect everything, Mr. Mannil admits with regret, he has limited himself to two main areas: works by contemporary South American painters and pre-Columbian art. In the second field he has acquired over 2,000 pieces since the day an Indian appeared out of the Costa Rican backwoods to offer him a ceramic tripod.

To be shown the collections by the Mannils themselves is an education, since Mrs. Mannil is vice-president of the Contemporary Arts Museum in Caracas. Cruz-Diez, Soto and Henry Bermudas, she explains, are among the best-known Venezuelan artists represented, but she shows many works by other South Americans: Nedo, Polesello, Obregon and some hangings in horsehair and wool by Olga Amaral, a Colombian weaver. Pre-Columbian objects have their own powerful atmosphere. The living room extends through glass doors to a terrace, but its main feature is a square glass vitrine, reaching from floor to ceiling. In it, arranged in five rows, are several dozen monolithic stone figures, posed on cement stands that raise them to heights of three or four feet, on a flooring of pebbles. "'The family,' we call them," says Mrs. Mannil. "I always think that one day I'm going to look in and see myself."

Everywhere—in corners, in perspectives, out on the terraces—are other equally well-placed objects. In the dining room, for instance, attention is focused on one of the best pieces in the house, a terra-cotta figure of a woman in labor, dating from about A.D. 600. One room, in which the Mannils sometimes take coffee or drinks, has wooden beams and joists exposed in the manner of an English pub, but instead of windows it has six oblong cabinets containing over 200 gold pieces. "Only two of them are doubtful," says Mr. Mannil, proud of having avoided the fakes so easy to come by. And at the lower level, below the reception rooms, is the pièce de résistance: a gallery with museum showcases in which are gold pectorals and brooches, jewels and jade.

All through the house are modern sofas, upholstered in bright red or Florentine brown leather, and these are from a shop in Caracas. And here and there are fits and starts of other collections that never quite came to complete fulfillment—notably a corner of Greek and Russian icons. In addition Mr. Mannil has a number of etchings and drypoints by an artist who was an Estonian contemporary of his, Eduard Wiiralt, a landscapist with a dazzling sideline in Bosch-like nightmares. His art admirably holds its own against the primitivism of the pre-Columbian culture that was conceived all those centuries ago.

The contemporary simplicity of Mr. and Mrs. Harry
Mannil's Caracas home, designed by architect Klaus F.
Heufer, offers a distinctive setting for an extensive pre-
Columbian art collection. PRECEDING PAGE: In the Living
Room, solemn-visaged figures dating from the 9th through
the 16th centuries create a community of monolithic forms.
ABOVE: A handwoven rug demarcates a conversation area
in the Living Room. The painting is by Carlos Rojas.

Along one wall of the Library, vitrines display richly decorated ceramic vessels made in the 13th through the 16th
centuries in Costa Rica. Other Costa Rican objects include a
ceremonial metate ornamented with bird forms, on the free-
standing pedestal, and, on the desk, a life-size stone head.

OPPOSITE: *A massive stone sculpture and a ceremonial stone ball, both from Costa Rica, share a tropical milieu in the lush indoor Garden.* OPPOSITE BELOW LEFT: *An Ecuadorian stone throne, which dates from A.D. 300–500, distinguishes the Terrace. Italian travertine flooring adds gleaming contrast.* OPPOSITE BELOW RIGHT: *Another smooth ceremonial ball ornaments a small fish pond.* ABOVE: *A Terrace setting emphasizes the earthiness of contemporary Guajira Indian pottery. Beyond, a broad vista encompasses the densely developed eastern section of Caracas and an airstrip, both nestled in a valley at the base of Mount Avila.*

A RARE SAMPLING OF AMERICANA

"You might call this old place my 'Bicentennial gesture,'" says interior designer Helen Partello-Hollingsworth of the eighteenth-century Connecticut farmhouse she took under her wing in 1976. As gestures go, this sudden immersion in Early Americana was as dramatic a departure from her personal tradition as can be imagined. Nurtured in the design climate of southern California, educated in European art schools, she had a reputation as a designer of elegant, soigné interiors. Now she was plunging into the cold waters of New England country architecture: simple, unadorned and homespun.

"I bought the house scarcely three months after moving myself and my business to New York," she recalls, "and I chose it more on instinct than on practical information about its pedigree. The land was beautiful but the house gave few strong clues as to what it could become. It had been remodeled three times since it was built in 1790, each time to the detriment of the structure. To bring it back to the proper beginnings turned out to be a huge undertaking. I had to become something of an archaeologist, taking away layers of debris to get to the treasure. As I wasn't entirely sure in those days what I wanted or how it should be done, I chose to do a considerable part of the work myself, learning as I went." Inside, the archaelogical spadework was equally tedious. Earlier tenants had added new carpet, wallpaper and paint without removing what came before. Peeling the layers was like unwrapping a mummy. Beneath, however, were plaster, chestnut floorboards, handpegged joinery and ornamental carvings—all part of the original structure.

The house was first built as a center-chimney Colonial, with all the bedrooms upstairs and a parlor, borning room, kitchen and other smaller service rooms downstairs. But long before the present owner took over, an old barn had been attached to the rear north wall to serve as storage space. She thought that the barn wing could make a delightful bed-sitting room. "I have since learned that this sort of informal arrangement was a common wintertime solution to living in the Northeast. People actually moved the four-poster down by the main fireplace to keep warm, and they were not shy about wrapping themselves up in the featherbed, even when visitors came. I sometimes do the same thing."

Once the house was on the way to rediscovering its past, the former Californian allowed herself to indulge in another new passion—collecting Early American furniture. "I was brought up on formal French and Italian furniture, and as a result I think I see this kind of country furniture with a special appreciation. I'm fascinated by its honesty, its uncluttered look." She admits to being more eclectic than many old-house enthusiasts. "I can appreciate collectors who specialize in buying only Connecticut furniture for an old Connecticut house, but I can't narrow my focus that much. I am fascinated by a great deal of Shaker furniture, and I also prize a number of pieces that originated in New York, Massachusetts and the Delaware Valley. I think they complement one another very well."

Now that she appears to have her house finished, is Helen Partello-Hollingsworth content with it? "I'm content to the extent that the experience of restoring and living in this place has been, and continues to be, personally and professionally rewarding. Just the doing of it has given me a precious new sense of self-sufficiency. I feel I can cope with any challenge that comes my way. But as for really being finished here, no. I expect to keep refining my taste and my collections, replacing good things with better ones the moment I find them."

A collection of American primitive furniture maintains the integrity of designer Helen Partello-Hollingsworth's 1790 farmhouse in Connecticut. PRECEDING PAGE: At the far side of the Dining Room stands a favorite piece, a timeworn painted blacksmith's desk. LEFT: Punctuating the Colonial clapboard residence is an unusual attic window added in Victorian times. TOP: The herb garden features an assortment of early-American favorites. ABOVE: Tin decoys nest among petunias beside an 18th-century dry-stone wall that could have inspired Robert Frost's line: "Good fences make good neighbors." A bluestone table permits alfresco dining.

PRECEDING PAGES: *Faithful to post-Revolutionary décor are the hand-stenciled wood flooring, whitewashed walls and contrasting painted wood detailing in the Living Room. The Shaker peddler's table, a sap yoke, a bull-shaped weather vane and early homespun blankets exemplify the stark aesthetic purity of the period.* ABOVE: *On the scrub-top worktable in the Living Room, a yarn winder evokes New England industriousness.* RIGHT: *Originally the kitchen and focal point of family life, the Dining Room perpetuates the feeling of hospitality. A long trestle table is accompanied by a Pennsylvania settee and chairs. The 18th-century cupboard displays pewter and Connecticut redware pottery.*

The Master Bedroom, formerly a barn, features an original blue-washed ceiling and hand-stenciled wall designs, after patterns by Moses Eaton. OPPO-SITE: A modern stove from Denmark complements the clean lines of the long Pennsylvania water bench and the pencil-post rope bed. ABOVE LEFT: A barn cupboard was once suspended from the ceiling to prevent mice from eating its store of potatoes. ABOVE: A schoolmaster's desk and a Vermont lantern are displayed in crisp juxtaposition. A sponge-dappled blanket chest reveals the inventiveness of the local artisans. LEFT: A New England cupboard in the Guest Room retains its original paint.

ETHNIC AND FOLK ART

At first glance, the brick Victorian residence of JoAnne and William Nicholson, in Washington, D.C. may not seem particularly unusual. But even from the sidewalk before the handhewn door there is the feeling that something here *is* different. Unlike neighboring houses, its windows have no draperies; instead, the sills hold primitive statues that seem to dance in the surrounding light. At the time the Nicholsons acquired the house, its location—a few blocks from the White House, where Mr. Nicholson was then appointments secretary to President Gerald Ford—was an advantage. It had another advantage, one that most buyers would consider an obstacle: Gutted by fire, nothing of the interior could be saved. "Which meant we could go in any direction we wished," says Mrs. Nicholson.

Now, few doors or walls divide one area from another. A bank of windows opening onto a terrace from the first level floods the plant-filled interior with light. Skylights over the three-storied continuous space and a hollowed-out cupola over the master bedroom seem to dismiss the Victorian exterior, creating a contemporary life of their own. At night the environment shifts once again, as lighting skims or accentuates different objects. To achieve the desired effects, the owners worked with architect Fred Klein and design consultant Alison Martin.

Mrs. Nicholson, who, as she says, "could pronounce dinosaur names before I could say regular words," was an avid collector of Indian artifacts while growing up in the state of Washington. She met her future husband while studying anthropology at the University of Nevada. William Nicholson had collected Indian rugs and the work of Alaskan Eskimos. After they were married, in 1967, they became interested in New Guinea artifacts. Their interests, travels and collections now include Af-

rica, Persia, Greece, India, the Far East—and Central and South America. "We never collect with the thought of where we will place an object," Mrs. Nicholson explains. "We feel a good interior is never finished, but keeps growing as we do."

The entrance hall is a friendly forest peopled with larger-than-life figures and images, all intent on telling their own stories. The faces of masks and statues stare from every direction. A mask with long straw hair looks over the shoulder of a sculpture of Adam. A crocodile head smiles back from over the front door, while an oversized parrot by Sergio Bustamante swings in its very own world of plants across the ceiling from a personable giraffe. "Each object has strength and makes a statement of its own," says Mrs. Nicholson. "Each one can be in a room with the others and yet not be diminished in any way. The American crafts are strong and light in feeling, yet whimsical. Nothing is abstract. We enjoy reality—with a touch of fantasy. And, in addition to carrying on visual conversations, all the objects have a certain color harmony."

Color, in fact, which ties together all the ingredients of the house, is Mrs. Nicholson's business. As president and cofounder of Color 1, an international consultation firm, she feels that "décor should start with the person. Many interior designers build a room around a sculpture or favorite possession, whereas I see the occupant as the focal point." One problem that couples create without realizing it, she feels, results from not developing an interior together. "If a husband says to his wife, 'Decorate the house any way you want,' and she does it without taking his tastes into consideration, he'll never feel a part of it. However, Bill and I, with the help of Alison Martin, created this house together. It's our work, and we're certainly happy with it."

In their Victorian residence in Washington, D.C., JoAnne and William Nicholson have fashioned a crisply contemporary setting for their collection of ethnic and American folk art. PRECEDING PAGE: A large New Guinea ceremonial crocodile basks on the chimney breast of the Living Room; to its right is a Guatemalan santo. The soft sculpture giraffe is by Andrea Uravitch. LEFT: Masks arrayed in the Living Room come from tribes in Africa, New Guinea, Mexico, Canada and the United States. They overlook a Berber rug, a fabric cylinder from India and a large triangular plaque from New Guinea. Near the window stands Adam, by American sculptor Myra Henry. ABOVE: On the Dining Balcony, an imposing warrior figure and a ceremonial shield, both from New Guinea, flank a Mexican cabinet.

117

LEFT: *The axis of the free-flowing interior is the central light well; on the Dining Balcony, beyond, an aura of mystery is enhanced by a blend of candlelight, diffused daylight and light projected through stained glass panels overhead.*
ABOVE: *A menagerie of imaginative animal figures lends endearing warmth to the Master Bedroom. Near the windows, an Ecuadorian polychrome parrot and a Portuguese leather kangaroo observe a soft-sculpture creature by Andrea Uravitch. Moroccan brass mirrors gleam above a Korean chest with butterfly-motif mounts. The polychrome totem is from New Guinea; the tapa cloth, from Polynesia.*

119

GARDEN OF ART

At Cala Ratjada on the island of Majorca, off the eastern coast of Spain, lies a garden with a double claim to uniqueness. It is the only large garden in Europe highlighting a single genus of flowering plants, bougainvillea, and it harbors a prime collection of modern sculpture, with works by Henry Moore, Barbara Hepworth, Max Bill, Eduardo Chillida and Antoni Tapiès—among many others. This wealth of modern sculpture and the bougainvillea so characteristic of the Mediterranean are found on a pine-clad hill beside the sea. Crowning the hill is *Sa Torre Cega*, "The Blind Tower," an Italianate residence recently redecorated by Carlo Ortiz. Its walls, inevitably, are covered with bougainvillea. The owner of the house and its twenty-acre garden is Don Bartolomé March, a member of one of the most prominent banking families in Spain.

Almost as strong as his passion for Majorca is Don Bartolomé's passion for collecting art and antiques. He is a collector by both instinct and inclination. Yet Don Bartolomé is quick to give credit for his unusual gathering of sculpture and flowers to his landscape architect, Russell Page. Indeed, it was Mr. Page who proposed to him the idea of making the Majorcan hilltop a temple to the genus *Bougainvillea* and to the modern movement in sculpture as well. But the owner himself had a clear purpose in mind: By juxtaposing the best in Spanish and world sculpture, he was making a direct and unambiguous statement. It was his wish to honor and inspire his countrymen, whose art had received so little encouragement during the Franco regime.

The idea of a sculpture garden, of course, is nothing new. From the Roman times—and no doubt long before that—few good country houses were complete without statuary, but a private sculpture garden on the scale of Sa Torre Cega is probably without equal in Europe today. It is a contemporary interpretation, on a rather more reduced scale, of the sort of sculpture garden created by the emperor Hadrian at Tivoli, for example, or the gardens at Versailles or that of the Spanish royal palace at La Granja, near Segovia. However, all these gardens are formal and the sculpture predominantly classical and representational. At Sa Torre Cega, for the most part, all the sculpture is abstract, and in the fullest sense the garden is an outdoor museum. Here no single piece need compete with another, and each work can be admired to best advantage—from every side and from every perspective. The sculpture is there to be touched and admired, and the garden setting provides for one rare surprise after another. Down paths and sometimes almost hidden by bougainvillea will be the arresting works of man—a white marble figure by the Cuban painter Cardenas, for example; a glistening totem head by Henry Moore; an arrangement of pivoted steel pipes, so contrived by José Maria de Labra Suazo that a movement of the hand can change it into a different, but related, design. The surprises are endless, and the arrangement is intriguing.

The problems in maintaining an organic art gallery are considerable. First of all, it is essential to see that nature itself does not overwhelm the sculpture, and then there is the special care that the bougainvillea plants require on this Majorcan hilltop. So Don Bartolomé March must watch his garden carefully, but he has succeeded admirably in nourishing both flowers and sculpture. It is his habit, for example, to add at least one new piece of sculpture each year, something that will reflect and enhance the quality of his collection. Like the bougainvillea itself, his is a living and growing collection of sculpture that can only improve with time.

120

Modern sculpture enriches the vast garden designed by landscape architect Russell Page for Sa Torri Cega, the Majorca home of collector Bartolomé March. PRECEDING PAGE: *Barbara Hepworth's* Otono *(left foreground) occupies a terraced clearing.* RIGHT: *Made of rotating stainless steel pipes, José Maria de Labra Suazo's kinetic sculpture can assume infinite aspects.* BELOW RIGHT: *Basque artist José Alberdi's stone* Oda al Greco *conveys a rough-hewn, totemic quality. The effect is intensified by the tree-studded setting.* OPPOSITE: *Spanish sculptor Chirino's untitled composition mingles bright color and strong form.*

123

LEFT: *The structural cohesiveness of Eusebio Sempere's untitled composition in steel imparts a sense of radiating power.* BELOW LEFT: *Henry Moore's undulant* Torso *basks in a clearing. Kleinia plantings underscore the work's organic volumes.* OPPOSITE: *A 1937 abstract composition by Max Bill shares a glade with other sculptures in the collection, including, at left, Chillida's* Alegoria de la Arquitectura.

RIGHT: *Sunlight and shadows mottle the gleaming surface of a sculpture by the French artist Pichet.* BELOW RIGHT: *An eight-foot tortoiselike creature of stone is by Ostero Besteiro.* OPPOSITE: *Large golden spheres seem to be suspended among 19th-century marble columns, in a work by Xavier Corbero. Like some plaything of the gods, the monumental sculpture dramatizes a clearing that overlooks the Mediterranean.*

ART NOUVEAU IN BRUSSELS

One of the choicest collections of Art Nouveau in the world today is to be found in Brussels. It belongs to Mme Anne-Marie Gillion Crowet, and the unique art, furniture and *objets* of the period have been brought together in her own apartment. Mme Gillion Crowet has limited her collection to a handful of the acknowledged masters of Art Nouveau, artists and craftsmen who created its unusual thrust with their devotion not only to nature itself, but to a poetic and symbolic interpretation of it as well—from stylized floral designs to luxuriant vines; from Louis Majorelle's furniture shaped like water lilies to the marquetry of Emile Gallé, all characterized by a profusion of curves.

With the eye of a perfectionist, Mme Gillion Crowet formed her collection by searching tirelessly for the unique works of the period, which lasted from the 1880s to the start of World War I. She has gathered examples of all the masters of Art Nouveau, particularly those of the School of Nancy. Actually, her only pieces not originating in that school are the work of the Belgian architect Victor Horta, who was a designer in the complete sense of the word. He created furniture, fabrics, rugs, staircases, lighting fixtures—even doorknobs and bellpulls. It was Horta's idea that the artist and the architect should be one, that interior details were an inseparable part of the design of any building.

On the other hand, the French School of Nancy was less rigorous in its concepts of total environment. Their designs for furniture, accessories and glassware fit more easily into a variety of backgrounds. These French artists, representing many different disciplines, formed themselves into a loosely defined "school," named after the town of Nancy, where most of them were born. Furniture made at Nancy was created from the finest and most exotic woods: rare mahogany, violet wood, West Indian hardwood and rose laurel, among others. Decorations were in silver or pewter, chiseled bronze or handworked steel. What drew Mme Gillion Crowet particularly to the work of Gallé was the exquisite use he made of natural forms. His love of nature, which he studied with a passion, shines forth in every one of his creations. In contrast, the furniture designed by Louis Majorelle was rather more architectural in form. His style was less emotional and instinctive, more logical and intellectual.

In assembling the unusual décor for her apartment, Mme Gillion Crowet had no desire to create period rooms. While retaining the basic architectural qualities of a contemporary apartment, however, she altered it subtly to conform to her collection. Wherever possible, she obscured rigid lines and substituted the contours so characteristic of the furniture of Gallé and Majorelle. And she has used colors in keeping with the Art Nouveau period: mauves, violets, beiges. While avoiding a literal re-creation, she has succeeded in suggesting the essence of an era. Perhaps she is proudest of the magnificent wallcovering of marble and ceramic salvaged from the fire that destroyed the Château d'Ardennes. These walls, commissioned by King Leopold II of Belgium, now grace the entrance hall of her apartment. The furniture in the hall came from the Hôtel Aubecq, in Brussels, built in 1899 by Horta.

Even though the apartment is filled with unique treasures, Mme Gillion Crowet rejects the idea that she is living in a museum. The atmosphere is quite the opposite. Everything has been arranged with consummate taste; nothing is excessive. There is a dreamlike quality, too, but joined with it is the sense of gaiety with which the owner has expressed the rare and philosophical style of Art Nouveau.

In her Brussels apartment, Mme Anne-Marie Gillion Crowet has gathered works by the masters of Art Nouveau. PRECEDING PAGE: *The ceramic fireplace by Muller in the Sitting Room symbolizes fire. The painting is by Jean Delville.* OPPOSITE: *The marble and ceramic wallcovering in the Entrance Hall was created by Belgian architect-designer Victor Horta, who also designed the sycamore furniture. The bronze ostrich is by Bugatti; the lanterns are by Gallé.*

Outstanding examples of Art Nouveau are displayed like sculpture in the Salon. The bronze-doré water lily furniture is by Majorelle. ABOVE LEFT: *A vitrine holds French and Belgian glassware and a Despret pâte-de-verre mask of Cleo de Merode.* ABOVE: *The bronze figure of dancer Loie Fuller is by Raoul Larche; glass pieces are by Gallé, Daum, Wolfers and Decorchemont.*

LEFT: *Works by Fernand Khnopff—a notable bronze Medusa and an esoteric painting—exemplify a collection of Belgian Symbolist art. The walls of the Salon have been subtly modified to conform to the sensuous contours of the designs. The gueridons are by Gallé.* ABOVE: *The large collection of French art glass includes a 1907 pâte-de-verre vase, at right, by Decorchemont, and six 1900–1904 vases by Gallé, among them a sea horse vessel.*

OPPOSITE: *Emile Gallé's versatility is demonstrated in the Dining Room by a marquetry sideboard, chairs without stretchers, faïence plates, crystal stemware and a marquetry table made after the designer's pattern. The allegorical paintings are by Khnopff.* ABOVE: *The painting,* Orphée, *is by Jean Delville, of the Symbolist School.* LEFT: *The Sitting Room desk with water lily mounts, the armchair and the bronze-doré lamp are by Majorelle. Enriching the setting are a luminous cameo glass shade by Daum and a bronze desk set by Tiffany. The painting is by Fabry.*

AN ADVENTURE IN ART

Perhaps no other collector has pursued twentieth-century art with such passion and personal involvement, or with such impressive success, as the late Peggy Guggenheim. It all began toward the end of 1937, when, after leaving her French painter husband, Lawrence Vail, she decided to open an art gallery in London. Marcel Duchamp introduced her to Surrealism and the Surrealists, and on his advice she bought her first piece of sculpture, *Shell and Head*, from Jean Arp. The gallery, named Guggenheim Jeune, opened with a show of Jean Cocteau and during its short career exhibited everything from Kandinsky and Tanguy to children's art. And, on the good advice of her then companion, the Irish playwright Samuel Beckett, Peggy Guggenheim collected. "As it was difficult to sell the work exhibited," she said, "I usually bought one painting or sculpture from each show, in order to console the artist. Without planning it, I started my own collection."

The gallery was a financial disaster, and in its second year she decided to open instead a museum of modern art in London. That project, however, was cut short by the start of World War II. Peggy Guggenheim moved to Paris—taking the list of art she had compiled for the museum. In Paris the list was revised with her friend Duchamp, and immediately she went on a buying crusade. She quickly collected two Dalis, a Man Ray, Giacometti's first bronze, two Antoine Pevsners, Léger's *Men in the City*, Brancusi's *Bird in Space*. From the collection of her couturier, Paul Poiret, she acquired her other great Brancusi bird, the *Maiastra*. With the Germans only two days out of Paris, Peggy Guggenheim sent her collection to be hidden on a farm near Vichy and fled to the south of France. There she aided numerous artists in their escape to America, until on July 13, 1941, she herself left for New York with her ex-husband, their two children, her new companion, Max Ernst—and her collection of artworks.

In New York she married Ernst and bought an East River mansion that was to become the hub of 1940s art. With a group of advisors that included André Breton, Ernst, Piet Mondrian, Alfred Barr, director of the Museum of Modern Art, and J. J. Sweeney, later director of the Guggenheim Museum, she opened her second gallery, Art of This Century. Every major Surrealist and Abstractionist was represented, as she impartially admired both movements. It was here that she introduced what is now popularly called Abstract Expressionism. Robert Motherwell, William Baziotes, Ad Reinhardt, Mark Rothko, Adolph Gottlieb, Clyfford Still, Hans Hofmann and Jackson Pollock all had their first one-man shows at the Art of This Century.

Despite her New York successes, Peggy Guggenheim longed to return to Europe. In 1947 she closed Art of This Century and moved to Venice, where she bought the unfinished *Palazzo Venier dei Leoni*. Its heavily stuccoed interior was, she explained, "like an elaborate bird cage and no place for modern art." So, much of the stucco came down, and an additional gallery was built on one side of the garden. Naturally, she continued to collect: Francis Bacon, Victor Vasarely, Matta, Sam Francis, Asger Jorn, Grace Hartigan, Eduardo Paolozzi, as well as Italian artists like Arnaldo Pomodoro, Tancredi, Giuseppe Santomaso and Piero Dorazio. In 1951 Peggy Guggenheim opened her Venetian palace and its sculpture garden to the public on a limited number of summer afternoons. And there, surrounded by her collection, she continued to receive the art world with the same buoyant enthusiasm, optimism and curiosity that kept "Peggy" and art mutually addicted for more than forty exciting and creative years.

PRECEDING PAGE: *In 1947, art doyenne Peggy Guggenheim chose Venice as her permanent abode, establishing herself and her incomparable collection of modern paintings and sculpture in the Palazzo Venier dei Leoni, a landmark designed by Lorenzo Boschetti in 1749.* LEFT: *The artworks in a Sitting Room are dominated by a Calder mobile and a René Bro painting. Bookshelves display a pair of Bambara antelopes and voluptuous glass sculptures by Jean Arp, while a Picasso vase occupies the low table.* ABOVE: *A Picasso painting, Giacometti sculptures and a Calder mobile make the Entrance Hall an artistic treasure trove.*

LEFT: *Senufo sculptures animate the Dining Room, where Archipenko's Cubist wooden sculpture rests beneath a Léger oil, at left. Muted earth tones color Ludwig Marcoussis's painting* Habitué, *next to it, and Jean Metzinger's stylized canvas between the windows. The furniture is 17th-century Spanish.* ABOVE: *Paintings by modern masters (from left to right) Jacques Villon, Robert Delaunay, Pablo Picasso and Juan Gris further enhance the Dining Room.*

ABOVE: *French artist Lawrence Vail, the collector's first husband, created the vase and bottle fantasies that adorn the Bedroom mantel. To either side, a copious earring collection is artfully displayed. A 19th-century Venetian corner cabinet and pair of armchairs project an air of engaging delicacy.*

ABOVE: *Two paintings by Joan Miró are evocative presences in the Gallery. Sculptures include Giacometti's first bronze, on the pedestal, and a polychrome Sepik River figure, in the corner. Visible through the arched window is a Romanesque wellhead in the garden.* ABOVE RIGHT: *Garden foliage surrounds a 1960 Max Ernst bronze sculpture entitled* In the Streets of Athens.

AT THE LIRIA PALACE

For more than a century and a half, the *Liria Palace* in Madrid has been the principal residence of the dukes of Alba, and today it is the home of the present duchess of Alba. The name of the palace, however, is derived from the Liria family, who initially constructed the building. The first duke of Liria was James Fitzjames, duke of Berwick. He was the illegitimate son of James, duke of York—later King James II of England—and Arabella Churchill, sister of the first duke of Marlborough. Philip V, first of the Bourbon kings of Spain, subsequently conferred upon him the additional title of Duke of Liria.

The Alba family itself, of course, goes back much further in history. It came into being in 1430 and, in fact, within a few years Don Fernándo Alvarez de Toledo was granted the title of Count of Alba, and his son Don García was made duke in 1472. The family flourished until the early nineteenth century, when the beautiful Duchess Cayetana de Alba died without issue. In consequence, because of a family relationship, all titles and properties of the Albas passed to their cousins, the dukes of Berwick and Liria. In the last third of the eighteenth century, the dukes of Berwick and Liria had built their own palace in Madrid, designed by Ventura Rodriguez. Thus, after the death of the Duchess Cayetana, in 1802, the Liria Palace became the principal home of the Albas. During the Spanish Civil War (1936–39) the palace burned, but most of its magnificent art, furnishings and collections were saved from the flames. After the war, Duke Jacobo, father of the present duchess, decided to rebuild the palace, though unhappily he did not live to see the conclusion of the work. With the new palace, a superb historical monument has been returned to the city of Madrid. The present duchess is named Cayetana, after her eighteenth-century ancestor. Like the earlier Cayetana, she is an only daughter, and thus similarly duchess of Alba in her own right. A great connoisseur and collector in the field of art, she is particularly knowledgeable about painting.

Perhaps the most notable and unique aspect of the Alba collection is that so much of it is closely tied to the history of the family itself. In the sixteenth century no less an artist than Titian painted the portrait of the Great Duke of Alba, a famous general who was governor of Flanders. And, of course, everyone is familiar with the passion Goya entertained for the eighteenth-century Duchess Cayetana. He painted countless portraits of her, and her features can be found in other works by the great Spanish artist. Along with the Goyas in the Liria Palace are many works by Winterhalter, court artist to the Empress Eugénie, wife of Napoleon III of France. Eugénie herself was a sister of the Duchess Paca de Alba, and Winterhalter painted many portraits of her that are now displayed in the Liria Palace. The renowned artists Sotomayor and Zuloaga, among others, painted likenesses of the parents and grandparents of the present duchess.

In addition to the great art specifically concerned with the family, there are innumerable canvases by the immortals of almost every period and almost every country. From Spain there is work by Velázquez and Zurbarán, El Greco and Murillo; from Italy, Fra Angelico and Raphael, Veronese and Guardi; from Holland, Rubens and Rembrandt; from England, Gainsborough and Reynolds, Romney and Constable; from France, Courbet and Corot—the collection seems without end. There can be no doubt that this palace in the heart of Madrid —with its paintings and furnishings, its handsome architecture and lovely gardens—is artistically the most important house in Spain, if not in the world.

ABOVE: *Built in the 18th century, the Liria Palace, in Madrid, has been the main residence of the Alba family since the 19th century. Duke Jacobo, father of the present Duchess Cayetana, began restoration of the imposing structure after it had been set afire during the Spanish Civil War; his daughter has continued to fill it with treasures.*
PRECEDING PAGE: *The luminous 1795 likeness of Duchess Cayetana, ancestor and namesake of the present duchess, provides the pièce de résistance of the Goya Salon. Other family portraits, including five canvases by Anton Rafael Mengs, are complemented by framed miniatures. The Empire mahogany and ormolu desk displays Chinese mineral trees, snuff bottles and* objets de vertu.

LEFT: *The majestic proportions of a marble-floored Reception Hall are ennobled by a Gothic tapestry; it is one of a series of nine, called* Troya de Grande, *that belonged in 1485 to the first duke of Alba.* BELOW: *The Italian Salon houses a princely collection of paintings by that country's masters. Exhibited are works by Fra Angelico, Perugino, Titian, Veronese, del Sarto, Raphael, Bellini, Maratti and others.*

The opulent Salon called Los Amores de los Dioses *is named for the central medallions of its roseate 18th-century Gobelin tapestries designed after cartoons by Boucher.* OPPOSITE: *Louis XV furnishings are illuminated by a pair of French porcelain urns, which conceal lighting, and a Rococo bronze chandelier. The fauteuils flanking the king-wood* bureau plat *are covered in Aubusson tapestry.* LEFT: *A Louis XV chinoiserie lacquer and ormolu commode holds Meissen porcelain figures.*

LEFT: *In the Salon of the Great Duke of Alba, Brussels tapestries, which appear to cover the walls like maps, evoke scenes of battles won by the Great Duke, a famous 16th-century general who was a governor of Flanders. Paintings and sculpture depict the Great Duke.* ABOVE: *The portrait of the Great Duke is by Titian.*